Seas Around the World

In and Around the Antarctic

The Antarctic is one of the world's most isolated and mysterious regions. Up until this century it remained largely unexplored. But today, with the aid of modern science, we have been able to open up large areas of snow, ice and freezing sea to study. Many countries now have scientific bases in the Antarctic.

In this book you will find out about the first brave explorers who risked their lives to bring back information about the region. You will be able to look at some of the strange and wonderful creatures that inhabit the land and waters of the Antarctic; and you will learn about the natural resources that the region has and the problems of pollution that threaten the wildlife.

In and Around the
Antarctic

Laurie Bolwell

Seas Around the World

In and Around the Arctic
In and Around the Pacific
In and Around the Antarctic
In and Around the Mediterranean

*This book is based on an original text
edited by Pat Hargreaves.*

First published in 1984 by
Wayland (Publishers) Limited
49 Lansdowne Place, Hove,
East Sussex BN3 1HF, England.

© Copyright 1984 Wayland (Publishers) Limited

ISBN 0 85078 448 4

Phototypeset by Kalligraphics Ltd
Redhill, Surrey
Printed in Italy by G. Canale & C.S.p.A., Turin
Bound in Great Britain by
R. J. Acford, Industrial Estate, Chichester.

The more difficult words contained in this book
are shown in **bold** type where they first appear
and can be found in the glossary.

Contents

A journey around the South Pole

The **South Pole** lies near the centre of the continent of Antarctica.
Antarctica is twice the size of Australia.
The coastline of Antarctica is 22,400 kilometres (14,000 miles) long.
Most of the continent lies inside the **Antarctic Circle**.

The land is covered by snow and ice all through the year.
At the edge of the sea the snow and ice end in huge ice cliffs.
Here is a picture taken on a very cold but sunny day.

During the long winter huge areas of the sea freeze over.
The flat area in this picture is frozen sea.
This man is a scientist who works in Antarctica.
His station is at McMurdo Sound (see the map on page 10).

Antarctica is called 'The Land of the Midnight Sun'.
On Midsummer's Day (which is in December) there is sunlight for
twenty-four hours.
But in winter there are long periods without any sun.

Antarctica was first seen in
1820 by a British seaman.
Explorers went to Antarctica.
Some stayed for the winter.
This cartoon is about how some
thought they spent their time.
The truth was much harsher.

This is an ice patrol boat.
It cuts through the ice.
The ice is 4 metres
(13 feet) thick.

The first team to spend
a winter in Antarctica
was British.
They sailed there in 1899.
Their ship was called the
Southern Cross.
They used sledges on the ice.
In 1911 the Norwegian Roald
Amundsen reached the
South Pole.
In 1933 the Americans also
went there.

Scientists study the rocks,
weather, ice and living things.
This scientist is taking a
sample of sea water.
He has made a hole in the ice.
He travels around on a sledge.

Here is a map of Antarctica.
Find the South Pole.
The sea around Antarctica is
the **Antarctic Ocean**.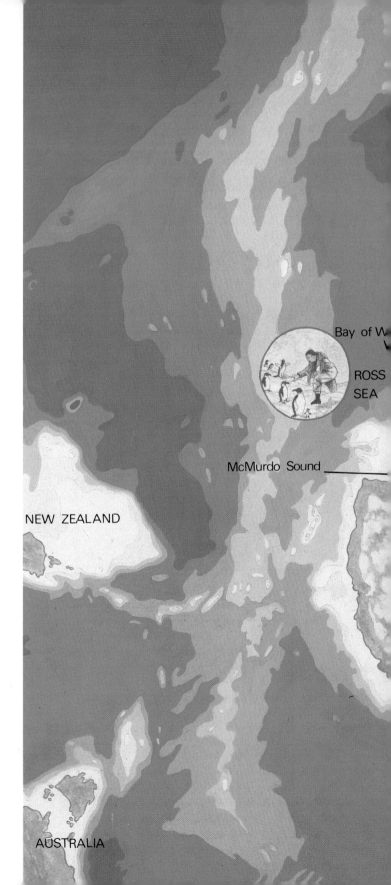

Three other continents are
shown on the edges of the map
– Australia, South America and
Africa.

Find the Falkland Islands and
South Georgia.
These are British islands.
The Falkland's war started when
the islands were invaded by
Argentines.

Parts of Antarctica are named
after explorers who discovered
them.
The Ross Sea and the Ross Ice
Shelf were named after Captain
James Ross.
The **Ice Shelf** lies between the
sea and the mainland.

Bay of W

ROSS
SEA

McMurdo Sound

NEW ZEALAND

AUSTRALIA

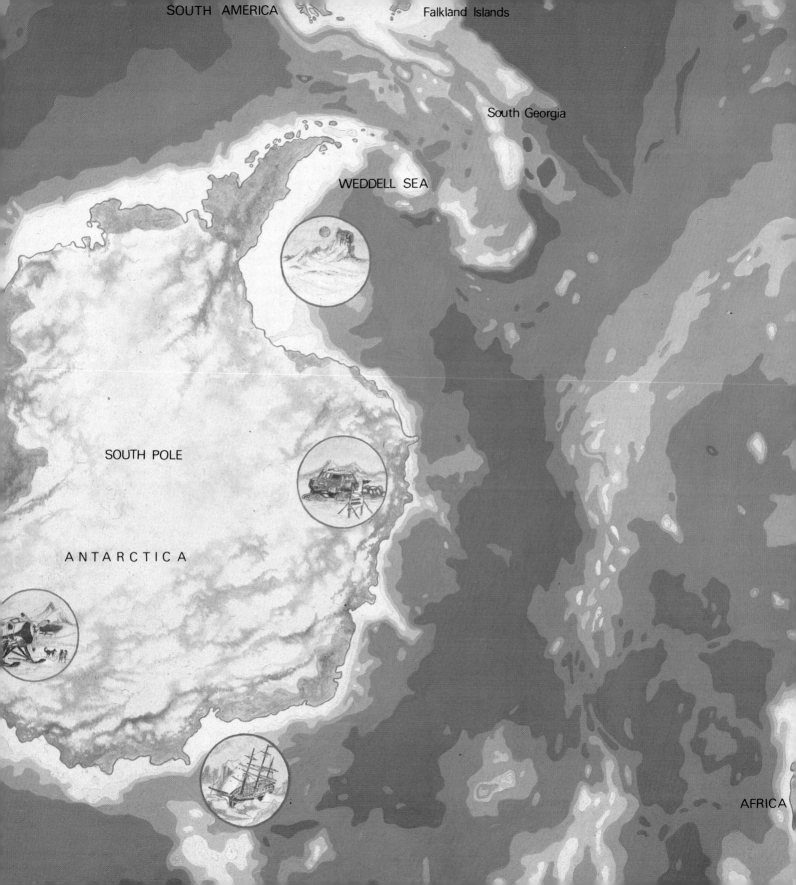

SOUTH AMERICA

Falkland Islands

South Georgia

WEDDELL SEA

SOUTH POLE

ANTARCTICA

AFRICA

The Antarctic Ocean

Here is a map of Antarctica and the bed of the sea.
If the water of the Antarctic Ocean was drained away this is
how it would look.
The continents and islands are shown in yellow.
Around the land areas lies the **continental shelf**.

The Pacific Antarctic Rise and Mid-Atlantic Ridge are chains
of mountains in the sea-bed.

There are also volcanoes
under the sea.
This volcano erupted in 1968.
Ash and lava shot up into
the sky.
A new island rose up.
It rose to 60 metres (195 feet)
above sea-level.

Compared with the age of most
of the earth, the Antarctic
Ocean is very young.
It has gradually got wider
over millions of years.

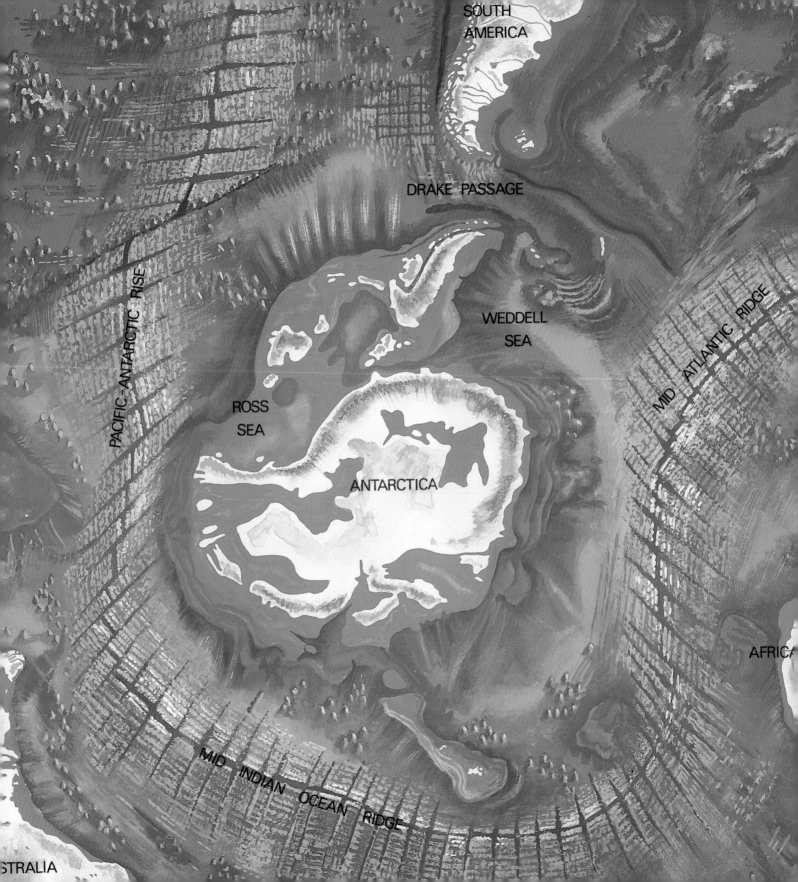

14

The continental shelf

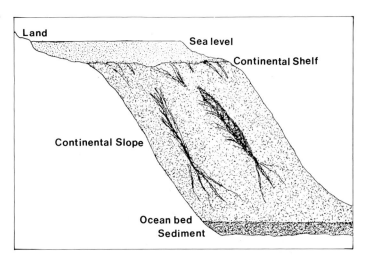

Near the land the Antarctic
Ocean is shallow.
This is because just beneath
the Ocean is a shelf.
This is the continental shelf.
It is smooth and fairly flat.

The continental shelf slopes down gently to a depth of
100 metres (330 feet).
Many fish and plants live in these shallow waters.
This is an underwater picture of marine life on the continental shelf.

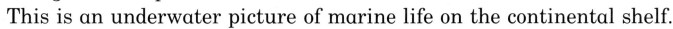

On the edges of the continental shelf the sea floor slopes downwards.
The slope is steep and the water gets very deep.
Sand and mud from the continental shelf slide down the slope
to the deep ocean floor.

The slope is very uneven in places.
There are great gorges and canyons under the water.

Beyond the **continental slope** is the ocean floor.
The ocean floor is quite flat and smooth.
It is covered with fine mud.
In places there are mountain ridges standing up in the cold dark waters.

Rocks and sediments

The mud and sand layer on the ocean floor is called sediment.
Most of it comes from the land.
The ice glaciers act like giant files as they cross the land.
They break off rocks, grind them down and carry the small
material to the sea.
These scientists are taking samples from the sea-bed.

Here is a **fossil** from the floor
of the Antarctic Ocean.
Scientists brought it up from
the sea-bed.
It is called an ammonite.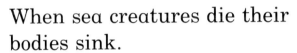
It is all that remains of a sea
creature that lived millions
of years ago.

When sea creatures die their
bodies sink.
Millions pile up to form a
layer of soft ooze on the
sea-bed.
They are pressed down by the
weight of the ocean.
They turn into chalk or
limestone rocks.
Some of the skeletons and
shells form fossils.

Ice ages

When the weather is very cold in winter, ice forms on ponds.
The ice melts when the weather gets warmer.
In the past this is how the great ice ages occurred.
Ice sheets grew when it was very cold but melted as it became warmer.

This is a fjord.
It is in Norway.
Once it was a valley on dry land.
The valley was cut by a **glacier**.

It was cut in the last great
ice age.
At the end of this ice age the
icecaps melted.
The level of the sea rose.
This valley was 'drowned'.
There are many fjords in
Norway.

18

All through the year Antarctica
is covered with ice and snow.
These are mountain tops in
Antarctica. ▶

Ice and the Antarctic Ocean

The Antarctic is higher and colder than other continents.
So the **ice sheet** only melts on the edges of the sea.
Icebergs break off from the edges of the ice sheet.
The icebergs are beaten and struck by the waves.
The sea cuts holes, caves and fantastic shapes in them.

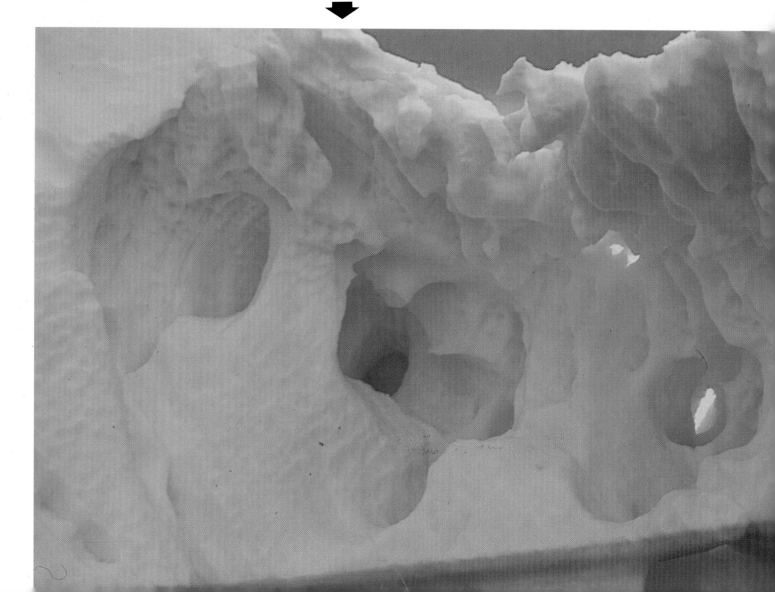

This picture shows ice cliffs.
They are part of an ice shelf.
This is in the Bay of Whales
in the Ross Sea.

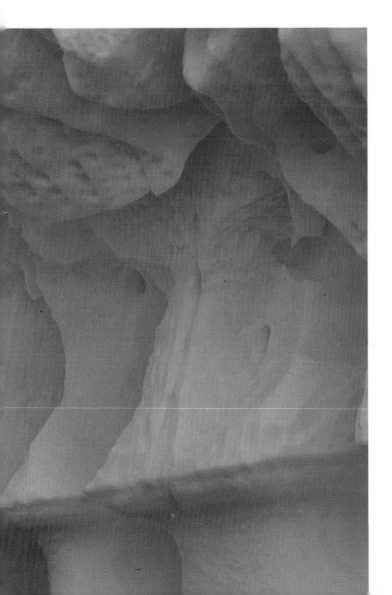

Find the Ross ice shelf on the
map on page 10.
This ice shelf is as big as Spain.
It stops ships reaching the
edge of the land.
Explorers had to travel over
the ice shelf to reach the
South Pole.
The edges of the sea freeze
in winter.
This is called **fast ice**.
Some drifts out into the sea.
It is then called **pack ice**.

This photograph was taken over eighty years ago.
It is H.M.S. *Discovery*.
It was the ship which took Captain Scott to Antarctica.
Here it is frozen into the fast ice in McMurdo Sound.
It could not break out of the ice for more than a year.

These men are looking over the bows of their research ship.
They are in the Weddell Sea surrounded by **ice floes**.
The floes are great chunks of pack ice broken off by waves.
The large flat area in the background is an iceberg.
It is a tabular iceberg – it has a flat top like a table.
A huge iceberg has enough water in it to supply London with
water for hundreds of years.

23

The first explorers

Captain Cook was the first to cross the Antarctic Circle.
This was over 200 years ago.
He did not land on Antarctica but other explorers followed.
They went to Antarctica in sailing ships.
This is the Bay of Whales.
Dogs are being used to pull men and supplies over the ice.

Today we can fly over the ice.
This photograph was taken
from a plane.
The mountain ridges are rocky
and bare.
Between them are glaciers.

These mountains rise to 3,000
metres (nearly 10,000 feet).
Above these mountains there
is a high plateau.
The South Pole is on that
plateau.

The dogs used in Antarctica
are called huskies.
They are tough and brave.
This dog is in a blizzard.
Snow has drifted over it.

One famous English explorer was Ernest Shackleton.
He tried to reach the South Pole in 1908.
He landed on McMurdo Sound and set up his base there.
This is his hut in McMurdo Sound exactly as he left it.
Look at the large stove and all the provisions.

This was Shackleton's ship *Endurance*.
It was caught between two ice floes in Antarctica.
As it was squashed in the ice the ship heeled over.

The crew had to leave the ship because it was so dangerous.
They had to live on the ice floe for three months.
At one time the floe split and the crew were on both sides.
The crack went right under one of the tents.

Shackleton and five men used an open boat to sail 1,100 kilometres
(685 miles) to get help.
They reached South Georgia and organized help for the others.

Today's expeditions

Early explorers wanted to make maps to show the South Pole.
They made records of icebergs, pack ice and the weather.
Then they began to study and collect sea plants and animals.

Here are some modern scientists at work.
On the left the thickness of the ice is being recorded.
The man on the right is taking samples from the sea floor.

The year 1957–58 was International Geophysical Year.
Many scientists went to the Antarctic to study the region.
Today, scientists from twelve countries still work in forty research stations in Antarctica.
One of these stations is right on the South Pole!

Some scientists study the weather and magnetism.
Others map the floor of the sea and study the sediments.
Ice, birds, plants and animals are being investigated by hundreds of scientists there.

Instruments have been moored in the sea and on the ice.
They move with the **currents** and as the ice melts.
Ships or satellites track their movements.
On the left the strength of the tide is being measured.
On the right rocks and sediments are being raised from the sea-bed.

Supplies for expeditions

This explorer is eating an egg. It is so big he holds it in his mug.
◀ It is the egg of an albatross. It takes about twenty minutes to cook. It is eight times bigger than a chicken's egg.

In the early days the explorers took their supplies with them.
Everything had to be packed in one or two small ships.
Today the scientists take much larger equipment.
Aircraft, tractors and lots of scientific instruments are needed.

The men need food, clothes and medical supplies for themselves.
They also need fuel to keep them warm.

All the stores are collected and packed in countries near Antarctica, such as New Zealand.
The supplies are flown to the scientific stations.
Today fresh fruit and vegetables can be eaten at the South Pole.

A modern **icebreaker** is able to cut through the thickest ice.
This one is breaking pack ice in McMurdo Sound.

This is 'Operation Deepfreeze' in Antarctica.
It is an American scientific expedition.
The scientists have stayed in Antarctica through the winter.
The ships have brought them supplies.

In spring aeroplanes leave Christchurch in New Zealand every day.
They land on thick ice in McMurdo Sound.
From there they fly out to the smaller scientific stations.
It is 1,360 kilometres (850 miles) from McMurdo Sound to the South Pole.

This U.S. Naval helicopter is landing stores at a small base.

Water movements

Look for Drake Passage on the map opposite.
It lies between Antarctica and South America.
It is the 'windiest place on earth'.
The powerful winds push along the water in the ocean.
Close to Antarctica the water moves eastwards.
Away from Antarctica the main movements are to the west.
This is a research ship going through Drake Passage.
The spray shows it is ploughing through heavy seas.

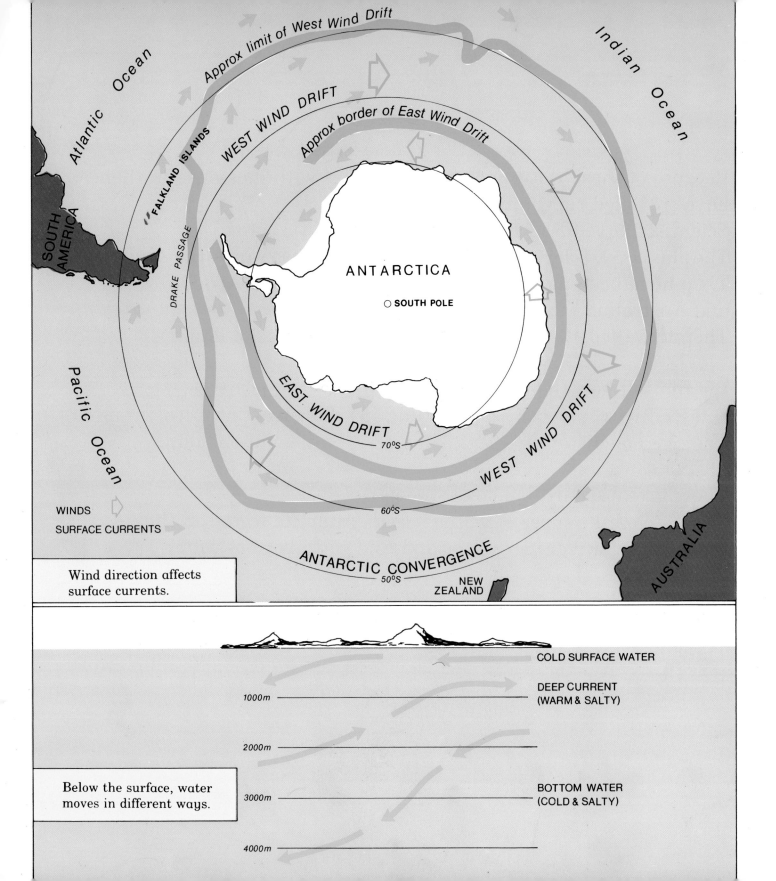

Atlantic Ocean

Indian Ocean

Approx limit of West Wind Drift

WEST WIND DRIFT

Approx border of East Wind Drift

FALKLAND ISLANDS

DRAKE PASSAGE

SOUTH AMERICA

Pacific Ocean

ANTARCTICA

○ SOUTH POLE

EAST WIND DRIFT

70°S

WEST WIND DRIFT

60°S

WINDS

SURFACE CURRENTS

ANTARCTIC CONVERGENCE

50°S

NEW ZEALAND

AUSTRALIA

Wind direction affects surface currents.

COLD SURFACE WATER

1000m

DEEP CURRENT (WARM & SALTY)

2000m

Below the surface, water moves in different ways.

3000m

BOTTOM WATER (COLD & SALTY)

4000m

Because of these water movements bottles with messages in them have travelled right around Antarctica.
Scientists have also experimented with plastic cards.
The plastic cards have been put in the water to see where they will end up.
They have been picked up in New Zealand, South Africa and Australia.
They travelled 12 to 16 kilometres (8 to 10 miles) a day.

We can tell how the currents move by tracking icebergs.
One iceberg was measured travelling 46 kilometres (29 miles) in one day.
The average distance is 15 kilometres (9 miles) in one day.

There are also currents below the surface.
There are three types of water – cold Antarctic water on the surface, warmer deeper water and cold salty bottom water.

In the Antarctic Ocean there is plenty of marine life.
This makes it a good fishing ground.
These fishermen have a good catch.

Waves and tides

Round-the-world yachtsmen like travelling west to east.
They know that the winds in the Antarctic Ocean blow mainly
in this direction.
The winds are very strong, especially in the **Roaring Forties**.
The strong winds cause very high waves which are dangerous.

These are huge icebergs in the
Antarctic Ocean.
They have been shaped
by waves.

They drift northwards from
Antarctica.
As they move they break up.
They are a danger to shipping.

The Antarctic Ocean is also
affected by **tides**.
Tides depend upon the 'pull'
of the moon and sun.

This ship is in great danger.
It is in a snow storm.
The gap in the pack ice
is very narrow.

Plankton and krill

Near the South Pole at midwinter there are twenty-four hours
of darkness.
At midsummer there are twenty-four hours of sunlight in a day.
So plants can only get the energy they need in summer.

The water of the ocean contains **nutrients** on which plants feed.
In summer millions of plants grow in the sea.
They are called **phytoplankton.**
This is what they look like under a microscope.

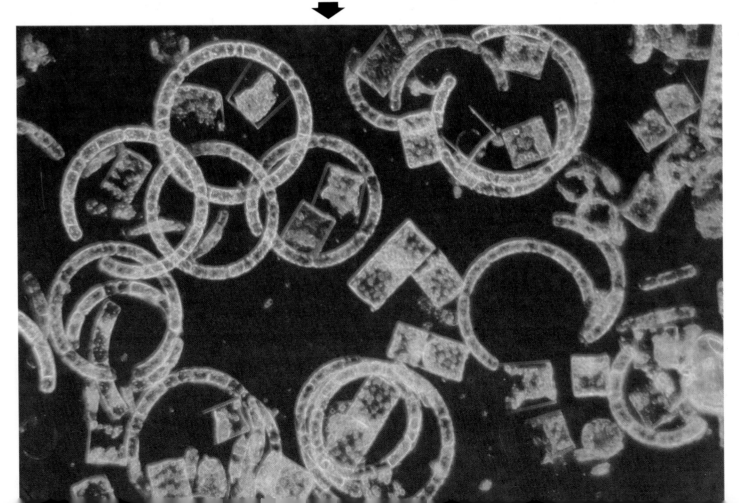

Phytoplankton is a rich source of food for fish and animals.
This is one animal which feeds on phytoplankton in summer.
It is the Antarctic krill.

Krill are **crustaceans** like shrimps.
They are often found together in large swarms.
Whales, birds and fish eat the krill.

There are also many tiny animals in the ocean.
They are called **zooplankton.**
Zooplankton include sea worms and kinds of jellyfish.

In spring the sea becomes thick with krill as the day gets longer.
A swarm may stretch for some kilometres across the sea.
The krill attract whales into the Antarctic.
They swim south for the rich food.
This is a southern right whale.

This is an ice fish which can live in very cold water.
Unlike other fish it does not have red blood pigment.
So its gills are white and not red.

Life near the sea-bed

Much of the sea-bed of the Antarctic Ocean is thick mud.
The mud is made up of the skeletons of millions of tiny sea creatures.
Many creatures live in and on this mud.

These animals are nemertine worms.
Some have long trunks to catch tiny animals for food.

You can guess what this animal is called – it is a sea spider.
It crawls around the sea-bed looking for food.

Sponges, sea anemones, crabs and starfish also live here.
They all have to be able to stay alive in low temperatures.
Some animals live only in the Antarctic Ocean.
Others live deep down in other oceans where it is also cold.

Whales

In summer the Antarctic is the feeding ground of the baleen
(or whalebone) whales.
As they eat the krill they store blubber (or fat) under their skins.
The whales are hunted for their blubber.
Here is an old picture of a whaling ship.

This is a Minke whale.
It is diving to deeper water.
Whales breathe air on the
surface of the ocean.
But they can stay under the
water for up to an hour.

The blue whale is the largest animal in the world.
This one has been landed at South Georgia.
There are very few blue whales left in the world today.

Seals

More than half the seals in the world live in Antarctica.
They catch their food in the sea and swim very well.
Their young are called pups and they have to come on land to have them.

This is a bull elephant seal which is the biggest kind of seal.
It is angry so the scientist is watching it carefully.
They can grow to between two and three tonnes in weight.

This is a leopard seal.
Leopard seals keep to themselves and are often found on ice floes.
They often prey on penguins.

There are six kinds of seal in Antarctica.
The most common kind is the crab-eater seal.
It does not eat crabs though, it eats krill!

Near the shore Weddell seals are found in large groups.
The rarest kind of seal is the Ross seal which lives on the pack ice.
Fur seals nearly died out because of hunting but are now protected.

Birds of the Antarctic

The best known Antarctic birds
are penguins.
Penguins cannot fly.
They swim very well.

There are many kinds of
penguins in Antarctica.
These are Adelie penguins.
They are lining up to dive
into the sea.

This is a beach on an island
in the Antarctic Ocean.
It is packed with penguins.
The females lay their eggs.
Male penguins hold the eggs
on their feet.
They do not have nests.
Parents carry their chicks until
they get too big.
Then the chick goes off to sea.

Another famous bird is the albatross.
Albatrosses are huge birds.
The biggest has a wingspan of 3½ metres (11½ feet).
Albatrosses may live for forty years.
This is a black-brow albatross.
It is guarding its chick.

A journey to the islands

This British scientist has to
cross a deep crevasse.
He is dragging his sledge over it.
It is a dangerous task.
He is on South Georgia.
It is an island in the
Antarctic Ocean.

There are many islands in the
seas surrounding Antarctica.
Some are lived on, like the
Falklands.
Some islands only have small
scientific bases.
Others only have seals and
sea birds living there.
All have long winters and very
stormy weather.

Many islands have wet, cool summers with mists and gales.
In winter there is plenty of snow and ice.

These gentoo penguins live on islands close to Antarctica.
They find their food in the open sea between ice floes.

Sailors feared the seas around the islands.
The high waves and great storms drove ships on to rocks.
Many ships were wrecked.

The Falkland Islands

The biggest group of islands in the seas around Antarctica
are the Falkland Islands.
They lie 480 kilometres (300 miles) east of South America.
There are two large islands and about 400 little ones.

This is one of the smaller islands.
This seaplane is landing supplies for the farmer.

Here is a typical scene on the Falklands.
The land is windswept and marshy with hills rising above the moors.

The Falklands were discovered about 300 years ago.
The French, Spanish and British settled there but only the British stayed.

The islands are divided into farms for cattle and sheep.
The British army now defends the Falklands from invasion.

Resources of the Ocean

The Antarctic Ocean has been harvested by many countries. The first harvest taken were the fur seals. They were killed for their skins. By 1820 they had almost disappeared. They cannot be hunted now and numbers have increased again.

Whales were also hunted. Factory ships stored the oil. Now there is a ban on hunting certain types of whales.

Today krill and fish are caught. Krill are used for pig-meal. 100,000 tonnes are caught each year.

Here is a whaling boat.
Dead whales are tied to the
side of the boat.

This is a krill trawler.
Krill must not be over-fished.
Many other creatures depend
on krill for food.
They will die without krill.

Countries of the world are now looking for oil under the sea. We know that there is oil, coal and natural gas in Antarctica. But we do not know how much there is.

The scientists are studying Antarctica very carefully. This man is taking a sample of ocean water.

It will not be easy to mine or drill Antarctica.

An important resource in the Antarctic is water. Icebergs are made of fresh water turned to ice. Some scientists think that icebergs could be towed away to dry lands to supply water.

DRYGALSKI ISLAND

LAND SIGHTED BY 1947 U.S. EXPEDITION

CAPE ANN

DESTINATION UNKNOWN

LAND SIGHTED BY NAZIS 1942

AMUNDSEN DEC. 1911
SHACKLETON HERE 1909
SOUTH
BYRD NOV. 1929

ROSS SEA

ANTARCTIC CIRCLE

CAPTAIN COOK HERE 1774

GRAHAM LAND

DESTINATION UNKNOWN

FIRST TRANS-ANTARCTIC FLIGHT 1935 (ELLSWORTH)

S. GEORGIA 1502

BELLINGSHAUSEN SEA

FALKLAND ISLES 1592

CAPE HORN

SOUTH   AMERICA

| GREAT BRITAIN |
| SOUTH AFRICA |
| NEW ZEALAND |
| U.S.A |
| FRANCE |
| RUSSIA |
| NORWAY |
| SWEDEN |
| CHILE |
| ARGENTINE |
| AUSTRALIA |

The future

The map opposite shows how many countries are in Antarctica.
Antarctica does not belong to any one country.
National expeditions work in different parts.
Seven nations claim parts of Antarctica.
Other nations do not accept these claims.

In 1959 twelve nations signed the Antarctic Treaty.
They agreed to work together in Antarctica and to use it
for peaceful purposes.

To protect plants and animals special agreements were made.
Specially protected areas have been set up.
They have had to think very carefully about the seas.
It is agreed that certain whales should not be hunted.
Fish and krill also have to be protected carefully.

This is one part of the world where the Americans and Russians
work together.
This has been a good example to the whole world.

The Antarctic Ocean is very clean at present.
If oil and coal are mined there will be problems with **pollution**.

▲

This is Flipper the penguin.
He is an American mascot.
He has his own uniform.

Scientists work hard in summer
Divers work from small boats. ▶
They explore the sea-bed, taking
marine samples to examine.

When planes are used on ice and snow they have skis.
This is an American aircraft.
It is taking off on skis from the South Pole.
The cloud is made up of smoke and ice fog.

Scientists still have many answers to find.
They do not know how many fish we can safely take from the seas.
This man is studying Antarctic cod to help find the answer.
We do not want fish to become **extinct** in the Antarctic Ocean.

This is a photograph of H.M.S. *Discovery*, the ship that took Captain Scott to the Antarctic on his first expedition.

Today you can see this famous ship moored on the Thames in London. The first person to have reached the South Pole was Roald Amundsen. Captain Scott got there on the 17th January 1912, only one month after Amundsen.

Captain Scott and his men all died on the return journey from the South Pole, but they are all remembered for their courage and endurance.

Glossary

Antarctic Circle   A line of latitude at 66°32' south.

Antarctic Ocean   The seas around the continent of Antarctica.

Continental shelf   The edge of a continent covered by shallow water.

Continental slope   A steep slope which joins the continental shelf to the ocean floor.

Crustacean   A sea creature with a hard shell and many legs.

Current   The flow of sea water in a particular direction.

Extinct   An animal or plant that has died out.

Fast ice   Frozen sea water found in sheltered bays.

Fossil   The remains or impression of a plant or animal in a rock.

Glacier   A huge river of ice which travels slowly down a mountainside.

Iceberg   A large mass of ice broken off an ice shelf. It is made up of fresh water.

Icebreaker   A ship which is specially built to break through pack ice.

Icecap A thick mass of snow and ice that permanently covers Antarctica.

Ice floe A chunk of pack ice broken off by waves.

Ice sheet A large area of snow and ice that covers the land.

Ice shelf Huge ice sheets on the coast. The shelf is fed by ice from glaciers.

Nutrients Food present in sea water formed by the decay of dead plants and animals.

Pack ice Frozen sea water which drifts with the waves and tides.

Plankton Tiny plants (**phytoplankton**) and animals (**zooplankton**) which drift through the sea.

Pollution Poisoning of sea water by oil, chemicals and waste matter.

Roaring forties Latitudes 40° to 50° south where there are fierce westerly gales.

South Pole The point at 90° south around which the earth spins.

Tides The rise and fall of the surface of the sea. Tides are the result of the sun and the moon pulling on the water.

Index

Picture acknowledgements

British Antarctic Survey 9, 14, 16, 17, 26, 29 (both), 31, 41, 43, 45, 47 (below), 49, 51, 53, 55, 56, 57 (above), 58, 59; Bruce Coleman, by the following photographers: Jen & Des Bartlett front cover, 23, 34, 42, 53, 54; Francesco Erize 6, 20–21, 38–39; Inigo Everson 57, 63, 65; M. P. Harris 50–51 (above); Gordon Williamson 47; Geoslides 19 (below); Tim Gill 10–11; Eric and David Hosking/D. P. Wilson 40; Anna Jupp 13; Keystone 19 (above); John Mitchell 15, 35; Seaphot 44; Bernard Stonehouse 7, 33; John Topham 8 (bottom), 12, 21, 24, 25 (both), 28, 30, 32, 37, 46, 48, 50–51 (below), 52, 60, 62, 64; Wayland Picture Library 8 (above), 22, 27, 39 (above), 66; Zefa *title page*.